HOW TO OVERCOME ANXIETY AND FIND PEACE

30 DAYS TO EQUIP FOR LIFE'S STORMS

ABIDE, #1 CHRISTIAN MEDITATION APP

ABIDE

How to Overcome Anxiety and Find Peace: 30 Days to Equip for
Life's Storms
Copyright © by Carpenters Code, Inc. 2017

Requests for information should be addressed to support@abide.is.

ISBN 978-0-692-99278-4 (hardcover)

Cover splash created by Harryarts - Freepik.com

TURN YOUR EYES UPON JESUS
Written by: GRIFFITH JONES, HELEN HEWARTH LEMMEL
Lyrics © Warner/Chappell Music, Inc., Kobalt Music Publishing Ltd.,
CAPITOL CHRISTIAN MUSIC GROUP
Lyrics Licensed & Provided by LyricFind

Creative writing: Kaitlin Wernet, Drew Dickens, Neil Ahlsten
Cover design, art direction, and interior design: Christina Ho
Editors: Neil Ahlsten, Dr. Ana Aspras Steele

CONTENTS

INTRODUCTION

All kinds of storms have blown through my life.
Growing up in a small Florida town meant afternoon
thunderstorms were always in the forecast. Each day
would start out the same way, with sunshine and
humidity, and just when it couldn't get any hotter,
clouds would begin to hover until the sky turned black.
While I learned to count on the trusty rays of heat, the
drenching afternoon rain and booming claps of thunder
always seemed to catch me by surprise. Whether it was
my mother calling from the doorstep, or my own
realization that I forgot an umbrella (again), I am
familiar with the urgency of "Quick! Get inside!"

Some summers were worse than others, with storms so
bad that I still remember their names — Gordon,
Andrew, and Dennis, to name a few. As their hurricane
winds howled into the night, I would lay afraid in my
bed tossing and turning to the sound of tree branches
cracking. I would pull the pillow over my ears, unable to
drown out the sounds. I couldn't silence my fears
either. Then came the prolonged power outages and
total darkness.

Whether a storm is raging outside my house or inside
my heart, I am no stranger to anxiety and suffering.
Anxiety's arrival is not as predictable as an afternoon

thunderstorm in Florida, but its ability to send me running for cover is just as strong. Thankfully, in Christ, I have found a safe place to hide — a shelter from the storm — when my days start to fill with dark clouds and I hear the warnings of "Quick! Get inside!"

As anxiety and suffering become part of our stories more and more, it is not always easy or automatic to remember that Jesus is the one who calms every storm. He is our shelter in small storms, our protection in big ones, and the light that guides us in the darkness. Once you discover this, you will also discover that His peace and His hope have come along too.

The heart behind this 30-day meditation on anxiety is that it will become a safe refuge for you to journal your thoughts and point you to the everlasting refuge you have in Christ. During the next 30 days, it is my prayer that you will experience the peace and power of Christ so profoundly that light will shine into the darkest areas of your life and make you feel more equipped and less alone in your anxiety. As you practice using Scripture each day to face and overcome your anxiety, fear, and suffering, this guide will teach you how to anchor yourself in Jesus, the true source of peace. These 30 days are designed to transform your anxiety into calm, your sleepless nights into peaceful rest, your anger into joy, your distractions into purpose, and your sufferings into hope.

As you respond to the questions in the journaling sections, feel the freedom to be honest with yourself and with God about what you are truly thinking and feeling. There are no right or wrong answers, and the more honest you are, the more open you will be to a transforming in God's powerful hands. Give yourself grace in the first few days to figure out the routine that works best for you, keeping in mind that the end goal is to experience God's life-giving peace.

Remember, inside the pages of this book your anxiety is welcome, your fears heard, and your hardships shared. Come as you are, eager to encounter the power and peace of Christ. Return whenever you face new storms and seek fresh shelter.

May the next 30 days be marked by His presence, His power, and His truth. He is with you, in this very moment. Let's begin!

A GUIDE TO CHRISTIAN MEDITATION

At Abide, we use three powerful, Bible-based exercises to help you meditate each day:

1. Refocus on God. You'll start each day by putting down all the distractions around you so you can slow down and recognize God's presence. Use the day's Scripture and devotion to refocus. This practice centers you on God's awesome truth and His power that's already at work around you.

2. Reflect with the Holy Spirit. You'll continue into the heart of your meditation time with three important questions. Seek profound insights from God about: 1) yourself and your situation, 2) about Jesus, 3) and about the people and things in your life that need attention. These quiet moments bring life-giving words that will renew your mind.

3. Respond through Jesus. You'll close each meditation with a powerful prayer from Scripture and a centering thought to take away. Ask for strength from God to do what He wants and take heart in the knowledge that God can do even more wonderful things than you can imagine. This gives the clarity, courage, and resolve to live in God's renewing power.

SECTION ONE
THE SOURCE OF PEACE

In this world, you will have trouble. But take heart! I have overcome the world.

John 16:33b

Jesus doesn't promise you a trouble-free life. Rather, He comes right out and guarantees that in this life you will have trouble. As hard as that may be to hear, I must admit that it's true. I have had many more tears and unspoken, lingering fears than you'll probably want to hear. If you feel the same way, welcome to the party. When Jesus sent out the invitation to His party, He said, "Go out quickly to the streets and lanes of the city, and bring in the poor and crippled and blind and lame." I've been down those streets and lanes. You may have, too.

In this first section, you will get to take an honest look at your troubles and the current storms in your life and practice what it means to "take heart." You'll learn how to begin to anchor yourself in Jesus, your most powerful source of peace who has overcome the world.

DAY 1: TROUBLE WILL COME

*But as for me, my feet had almost stumbled, my steps had
nearly slipped.*
Psalm 73:2

I chipped my two front teeth when I was learning to ride a
bike. Following the hours and hours my dad and I spent
practicing around and around our neighborhood cul-de-
sac, I was ready to take off the training wheels, or so I
thought.

My dad taught me everything I needed to know, from
balancing to turning, to what to do if I fell off my bike. And
while I wanted to heed that last bit of instruction with a
grain of salt and take on my neighborhood streets like my
own personal Tour de France, the last thing he taught me
is what I needed to learn the most: what to do when I fell
off, not if.

My dad didn't promise me that I wouldn't fall; he promised
that he would be there when I did. So, when I found myself
turning my bike a little too sharply and landing flat on the
ground, I didn't feel betrayed, I felt cared for.

Maybe you feel betrayed when storm clouds suddenly roll
in. Maybe you wonder if God still cares for you when your
feet almost stumble and your steps nearly slip. You were

riding your bike confidently through life, just sure that harm couldn't catch up to you. But it did anyway, landing you flat, with chipped teeth and cracks everywhere else in your life, too.

Remember, God promised that trouble would come, but He also said that His presence would never leave you.

Take an honest assessment today of where you are in your bike ride through life, of the trouble that has already come and the clouds that loom in the future. Then look again at what Jesus has to say about trouble. Claim the confidence and hope He has promised in John 16:33.

GO DEEPER

1. How do you feel about the promise that trouble will come? What hesitations do you have about believing it?

_____

_____

_____

_____

_____

_____

_____

GO DEEPER

2. What past, present, and future troubles stand out the most
   to you? How does it feel to know they don't surprise God?

Dear loving Father, thank You for the things You have already given me that sometimes I fail to see. In You, I am loved. In You, I am accepted. The title You have given me — "Your child" — exceeds any amount of praise and peace I could receive from the world. End my search, dear Lord, to find praise and peace apart from You and Your truth. Help me to live from the confidence I find in being called Yours. Because I am Yours, I can look to You for approval and love when I fall or forget who I am. Keep my feet from stumbling, for You, God, are my guide and my refuge. May I live fully loved because of everything Your Son has already done for me. May I live freely knowing that when my feet slip, You are there. Thank You that You will never leave me. Amen.

You are already fully loved, wholly accepted, and completely chosen.

DAY 2: JESUS THE PEACEMAKER

For there is one God, and there is one mediator between God and men, the man Christ Jesus, who gave himself as a ransom for all, which is the testimony given at the proper time.

1 Timothy 2:5-6

What are you good at making? Food? Friends? Photographs? The things people make never fail to amaze me. I am fascinated by makers of all kinds — artists who use paint to tell stories, inventors who experiment to solve problems, and musicians who create inspiring songs. But despite all of our skill and imagination, can any of us make perfect peace? Can you?

Jesus claims that He has made perfect peace. By giving His life as a ransom for us, He mediates between the trouble in your life and the perfect peace of God.

Jesus can heal every unrest in your life — the situations that make you anxious, the events you're unsure about, the times you don't feel in control.

Jesus takes you to God's peace — the love and power that calm the storms of any circumstance because He is in control.

Jesus doesn't just help solve our problems. Jesus is the

solution. He does more than sit and listen — He gives His life to end the conflict, to return you to the perfection of God in spite of your own imperfections. Jesus stands between your unrest and God's peace as a middleman — a go-between who calms the waters for us.

Jesus reconciles the tension between your anxious thoughts and God's unchanging truth. Thanks be to Him.

GO DEEPER

1. Imagine Jesus taking your hand and walking you away from your present unrest to His true rest. How does it feel?

_____

_____

_____

_____

_____

_____

_____

_____

_____

_____

_____

_____

2. How does the image of Christ as your peacemaker impact the way you view your anxiety? Why is that the case?

_____

_____

_____

_____

_____

_____

_____

_____

_____

_____

_____

_____

_____

_____

_____

_____

_____

Jesus, You are the one and only peacemaker. Thank You for being a mediator between the true perfection of God and my deep imperfections. Because of You, I can find peace. Because of Your work on the cross, I can see hope at the end of my fears. Help me to look to You when I am anxious, when it seems like nothing is within my control. Show me that You are in control and remind me that I can trust You and Your love for me. Thank You for who You are. In Your name. Amen.

Jesus came to give you the peace you seek.

DAY 3: FIX YOUR EYES ON CHRIST

My eyes are ever toward the Lord, for he will pluck my feet out of the net.
Psalm 25:15

I learned about seasickness the hard way — on a small fishing boat in the middle of the ocean. It was the morning after an especially intense storm, but my grandfather and I were determined to catch some fish anyway. Unfortunately, the waves weren't the only things churning unhappily. But, thankfully, a few hours into the trip, I also learned the tried and true fisherman's trick to preventing and overcoming seasickness: look to the horizon. Although it may seem counterintuitive, focusing on a distant, still object helps you feel more stable, even on a rocking ship. As I looked to the intersection of sky and sea, I started to feel much better.

The same is true for you, no matter how rocky your circumstances may be. Fixing your eyes on Christ, who is always steady, forever constant, and eternally loving, is the only true way to find peace. Turning your eyes to Him doesn't remind Him to resume His position at the wheel; rather, it reminds you that He has been at the wheel all along. Although you may feel ungrounded and helpless, He hasn't moved. He's been here all along.

Thank God for the steadiness and surety of His presence today. Pray these favorite hymn lyrics as a reminder to look to Him:

"Turn your eyes upon Jesus, Look full in His wonderful face;
And the things of earth will grow strangely dim
In the light of His glory and grace."

GO DEEPER

1. Visualize fixing your eyes upon Jesus in this moment. What is His reaction to your rocky circumstances?

_____

_____

_____

_____

_____

_____

_____

_____

_____

_____

_____

GO DEEPER

2. Psalm 25 says, He will "pluck my feet out of the net." What does this mean to you?

_____

_____

_____

_____

_____

_____

_____

_____

_____

_____

_____

_____

_____

_____

_____

_____

_____

_____

_____

_____

_____

_____

God, You never leave me. Like a good Father, You watch over me constantly, even when I forget You are there. Today, help me to fix my eyes on You and to reflect upon Your steadiness, knowing You never move from Your throne. I can count on Your love and trust in Your presence. Give me eyes to see You, especially when I am tempted or challenged. As the psalmist says, "Pluck my feet out of the net," and let me walk in the way of truth and righteousness. Amen.

Christ is with you, and Christ is for you.

DAY 4: GOD'S PROTECTION

Trust in the Lord forever, for the LORD GOD is an everlasting rock.

Isaiah 26:4

Over the years, our group of neighborhood kids eventually outgrew the game of Hide-and-Seek and traded it in for a different game to play in the dark — Sardines. If you've never played, it's like Hide-and-Seek, only in reverse. Instead of only one person doing the seeking and everyone else doing the hiding, in Sardines, only one person is hiding, and the rest of the group goes looking for the person who is hiding. The first person to find the hidden person stays hidden too. By the end of the game, the entire group is hiding in the same place, crammed together like sardines, and only one person is left looking.

Imagine what it's like being that final person who is left doing the looking. You've exhausted every possible hiding place, and you still can't find your friends and their hiding place. By now, you are starting to get totally frustrated looking for everyone.

It can be a similar experience with problems in your life. Your problems pile up; they feel all crammed together, like sardines, your frustration is mounting, and you still can't find a solution. You want to hide, too, but there aren't any more places left to hide.

It would be a recipe for despair, if it were true. But it's not true. Your desperate search, no matter what you're searching for, ends here, with God. His love stands to protect you, to guide you, to welcome you in, and to be your true hiding place. He is the only one who can be trusted to sort out your problems for you, to fight your battles, to find your solutions, and to lead you to safety. He is the one to hold you close, when everyone else has scattered.

Behind God's love, nothing can destroy you.
Behind God's love, He will redeem and restore you.
Behind God's love, you are watched over and protected.
Praise the Lord, for He is your hiding place.
Trust in Him forever.

GO DEEPER

1. What do you hide behind when you need protection? In whom or in what do you place your trust?

---

2. Visualize hiding behind a colossal, everlasting rock, where no one or nothing can get to you. Pray to God, asking for this image to transform your trust in Him.

_____

_____

_____

_____

_____

_____

_____

_____

_____

_____

_____

_____

_____

_____

_____

_____

_____

Dear Lord God, I confess that there are many things in my life that I find reliable and good. There are many people in my life that I lean on when my problems pile up, based on their good character, their abilities, and their strength. I thank You for these people in my life that I can trust. But, rather than letting my trust rest solely on them, may I look to You, my one true trust. You are the source of all good, all honesty, all ability, all strength, and all truth. Help me to trust confidently in You as my fortress, my shield, my banner, and my everlasting rock. I will forever be able to rely on You for love, forgiveness, and protection. Today, remind me of Your protection and love, and grow my trust in You. In Jesus' name. Amen.

God and His love will always protect you.

DAY 5: THE GOSPEL IS PEACE

Do not be anxious about anything, but in everything by prayer and supplication with thanksgiving let your requests be made known to God. And the peace of God, which surpasses all understanding, will guard your hearts and your minds in Christ Jesus.

Philippians 4:6-7

Anxiety is the friend nobody invites to dinner but who somehow always finds out when you're having a party. He barges in the door without a dish to share, and greedily fills up his plate, even going for seconds, leaving no leftovers in sight. Long after all the other guests have left, he lingers into the night, keeping you awake and on edge, wondering if he'll ever leave.

Anxiety doesn't head for the door the moment he realizes you want him gone. Sometimes it feels like that makes him want to unpack his suitcase and move in.

Philippians 4:6-7 is one of the most-quoted Bible verses in relation to anxiety; yet at times it can be very frustrating trying to obey its command, "Do not be anxious about anything." If anxiety is paying you a visit, you know how hard it is to get rid of him. It's certainly not as easy as just telling it to go home.

If your anxious thoughts feel out of control, there is a solution. In Christ, you have been given two powerful tools to combat anxiety — something to do and something to receive.

First, something to do: pray and make your requests known to God. Tell Him all your fears and also all your thoughts about the anxiety. Ask Him to remove your anxiety and replace it with His truth.

Second, something to receive: accept God's peace. If you didn't have a need for it, He wouldn't have given it. God's peace is greater than any fear and any anxiety. Remember, you don't need anxiety to leave you before you can receive God's gift of peace. Just ask God for His peace and let yourself receive it. Allow His peace to come in and overpower your anxiety. This will steady your heart and mind in Christ Jesus.

GO DEEPER

1. What worries you? What are you most anxious about today? Meditate on God's unbelievable peace from Philippians 4.

----

2. Picture God's peace guarding your heart and mind. What is it protecting you from? How is God's power driving out storms to bring you calm?

_____

_____

_____

_____

_____

_____

_____

_____

_____

_____

_____

_____

_____

_____

_____

_____

_____

_____

_____

Dear God, I am worried, about things I can't control, people I love, and things I don't even know about yet. Yet, You, God, sit on Your throne in heaven, and You hold all things in the palm of Your hand. You know all things, and You are weaving everything together for Your good purposes. Right now, I hand over my anxiety to You. Take it, Lord. Replace it with a faith that fully trusts Your goodness. May Your peace guard my heart and mind in Christ Jesus. Thank You for Your grace and love. Flood my soul with peace, dear God. In Jesus' name. Amen.

Anxiety can remind you of your need for the gift of God's peace.

SECTION TWO
REST WELL IN JESUS

And he awoke and rebuked the wind and said to the sea, "Peace! Be still!" And the wind ceased, and there was a great calm. He said to them, "Why are you so afraid? Have you still no faith?" And they were filled with great fear and said to one another, "Who then is this, that even the wind and the sea obey him?"

John 16:33b

Your rest is deeply important to God. It's a key part of God's plan. God tells you to rest in His presence by stopping your work and your chores to take a Sabbath. God Himself rested on the seventh day of creation. Resting in God is not a means to some higher goal; it is the goal.

When Jesus and His disciples were in a small fishing boat on the Sea of Galilee, a violent storm hit. Jesus was sound asleep. His disciples, terrified that they were going to die, woke Him up. Jesus immediately rebuked the wind and calmed the seas, then He asked His disciples why they were afraid, why they lacked faith. Jesus had great faith, and He rested soundly in God's presence. You can learn to rest like this, too. It takes a faith that only comes from knowing the awesome power of the God who calms the storms. Let's practice how to rest well in Jesus.

DAY 6: STOP AND REST

Be still, and know that I am God. I will be exalted among the nations, I will be exalted in the earth!

Psalm 46:10

Most mornings, the first thing I do after my alarm goes off is count the hours until I can return to my bed. It's the most safe and comforting place I know, and when I wake up under a pile of blankets, the last thing I want to do is step foot on the cold floor and face everything that waits for me outside.

It's a stark contrast — going from sound and refreshing sleep to a hectic schedule packed with uncertainty and nothing but coffee to aid the transition.

The transition from resting in God to relying on yourself is even worse, and much more painful. Sometimes, without even realizing it, you can shift from trusting in the power and safety of God's goodness to trusting in your own plans and abilities. The result is usually burn out, not just of our bodies, but also of our souls.

The phrase "be still" in Hebrew is *raphah* and is better translated "cease striving." It means to relax, sink down, and allow things to drop. Psalm 46:10 teaches us to rest well — cease striving — and remember that He is God.

Know He is God, who is in control and can be trusted.
Recognize He does not require your striving.
Notice the way He holds all things together.
See the work He wants to do *through* you, not the work
you think He demands of you.

Don't strive after the things of the world. Strive for the
rest you can only find in God.

GO DEEPER

1. In what ways are you relying on yourself instead of
   on God?

GO DEEPER

2. What would it look like to trade in your striving for being still? How would it feel?

_____

_____

_____

_____

_____

_____

_____

_____

_____

_____

_____

_____

_____

_____

_____

_____

_____

_____

_____

Dear God, when I rest, it helps me to know and trust You more. Many times, I find that I am even at peace with my enemies when I am at peace with You. You have already given me Your peace, and You will continue to do so, no matter what I face. Seal it on my heart, Lord, so that I will know You more and glorify You greatly. In this world there is tribulation, but You have overcome it all so that I can be still and know that, indeed, You are God. There is no reason for me to be anxious or worried because I can bring every concern and fear to You in prayer and thanksgiving. Grant me Your peace that passes all understanding — a peace that will guard my heart and mind through Christ. It's in His name that I pray. Amen.

Strive to rest in God.

DAY 7: WHAT YOU CAN HANDLE

*No temptation has overtaken you that is not common to man.
God is faithful, and he will not let you be tempted beyond your
ability, but with the temptation he will also provide the way of
escape, that you may be able to endure it.*

1 Corinthians 10:13

If I ever wonder how clumsy I am, I can look no further than
to the scar on my foot. I was ironing a shirt, in a hurry, and
before I knew it, the hot iron fell to the floor, and I bet you
can guess where it landed. *Ouch.*

Still in a hurry, I immediately did what I thought was best —
covered the burn with an ice pack. I know now that is the
worst thing you can do to a burn. *Double ouch.*

Although their intentions may be in the right place, people
can be very good at making things worse with their words.
When real tragedy strikes and our despair burns through us,
even the closest, most well-meaning friend can say things
that will make our hurt even worse, things like "God will
never give you more than you can handle." *Ouch.*
Double ouch.

Here's the truth: God will often give you more than you can
handle. This is not an oversight on His part, or something He
does to taunt you or cause you more pain. In fact, He is the

only one who can heal the scars left by your pain. God will often give you *more* than you can handle, but never more than He has already handled on the cross for you. Pain and grief and temptation will come, but they will never take Him by surprise, and they will never be too much that He cannot redeem it all for His good purposes for you. You will never be left alone in your worst-case scenario. Jesus is there with you in the worst trials and temptations to lift you up in His arms and walk you across the waters.

GO DEEPER

1. When have you faced a great temptation or tragedy or something you couldn't control? Where was God during that time?

_____

_____

_____

_____

_____

_____

_____

_____

_____

GO DEEPER

2. How does it make you feel to know that there is no emotion or temptation or situation you face that Christ cannot relate to?

_____

_____

_____

_____

_____

_____

_____

_____

_____

_____

_____

_____

_____

_____

_____

_____

_____

_____

Great God, You are mighty. You set the earth on its axis and the planets in orbit. You scattered the stars in the sky and separated the land from the seas. You know everything, and You have the power to do anything. Right now, I ask that You would give me strength. Help me through this hard season of life with Your wisdom and endurance. Let me fix my eyes on Jesus, the author and perfecter of my faith, as I persevere.

God handles what you can't.

DAY 8: LAY IT DOWN

"Come to me, all who labor and are heavy laden, and I will give you rest."
Matthew 11:28

Grocery shopping makes me very ambitious. No matter how many heavy bags of groceries I have, it is always my goal, without exception, to make no more than one bag-carrying trip inside the house. I've gotten pretty good at hanging too many plastic bags on each arm and balancing the weight until I get to the front door; but then comes the most challenging part of all: finding my keys. And just when I think I can do it all, one small movement is all it takes to send all the bags crashing to the ground — the milk jug splatters, the bag of fruit is bruised, and the potatoes are rolling down the street. Making a mess is the typical result when I try to carry too much on my own.

The only way to ensure the bags make it safely inside to the kitchen counter is to make more bag-carrying trips from the car and lay them all down before opening the door. After all, I was never meant to carry that many bags on my own in the first place. You weren't, either.

Whatever you carry, whatever it weighs, Jesus can help. He didn't just come to carry one of your bags to make your journey a little more pleasant — He came to carry them all. Psalm 68:19 tells us that He is our Burden Bearer. He came to take the cloudiness of the unknown, the downpour of your sadness, and the heaviness of your grief. He came because He knew you couldn't carry everything by yourself. He came to give you rest. Practice laying it all down before Him today.

GO DEEPER

1. What in your life is broken or most burdensome? Are you carrying too much on your own? Meditate on Matthew 11 and Psalm 68:19 and imagine laying down your burdens.

_____

_____

_____

_____

_____

_____

_____

_____

_____

_____

_____

_____

GO DEEPER

2. Journal a few words to describe the burdens you released to Jesus today. How did it feel?

_____

_____

_____

_____

_____

_____

_____

_____

_____

_____

_____

_____

_____

_____

_____

_____

_____

_____

Sovereign Christ, You are Lord of heaven and earth. You sit at the right hand of God, and You know everything about the circumstances I face. Every detail of my life has been entrusted to You. You are God, so I can stop trying to carry and control everything. I can stop trying to make everything perfect. Right now, I ask that You would search my heart. Show me the things that I am holding onto in vain. Help me to let go. Help me to trust You with my whole heart and my whole life. You know the plans You have for me, God. Grant me the wisdom to recognize the things that are worth my time and resources; give me the diligence to work hard for the things that really matter; bless me with the faith to say in my heart, "Your will be done." In Your name. Amen.

Nothing of yours is too heavy for Christ to carry.

DAY 9: WEARY AND HEAVY LADEN

You are my hiding place and my shield; I hope in your word.
Psalm 119:114

Some families play board games to pass the time, while mine mainly just tries to find the cat. Ever since she was a kitten, she has loved nooks and crannies of all shapes and sizes. Not even an hour after we brought her home, the whole family became a full-fledged search party in disbelief that we'd already lost our new pet. Thankfully, she was under my dresser.

Now, when we can't find her, she is usually just resting happily in one of her favorite hiding places, from the box underneath the bed to the spot on top of the refrigerator. This is the same type of refuge you have in God. With the Lord as your hiding place, you too can rest happily in a safe place.

In ancient Israel, God created refuge cities for those who had been wrongly accused where they would be kept safe, cared for, and protected from harm. In these refuge cities, their weariness could be put to rest and their burdens could be laid down.

God's heart is still to provide a safe place of rest for you as His child. He wants to be your covering from the storm, your shelter from the winds, and your safe harbor from the raging seas. When you hide in Him, your fear turns to joy, your trouble turns to calm, and your brokenness turns into restoration. May you only be found hiding behind the strength of your Creator when the trials come.

GO DEEPER

1. What does this passage in Psalm 119 tell you about God? How has He shown Himself to be a hiding place for you?

_____

_____

_____

_____

_____

_____

_____

_____

_____

_____

_____

_____

GO DEEPER

2. When you feel burdened or fearful, where do you go?
   Imagine God as your city of refuge. Journal about it.

My refuge and shield, help me hide myself in Your presence now. Don't let my heart be fooled into thinking that anyone or anything else can comfort, fulfill, or shelter me. Only You can, Lord. Expose the idols in my life, the things and people I lean on to make myself feel better instead of coming to You. Help me to run to You as my true hope, shelter, refuge, and God. You care for me as a Father cares for His child. You love me with an everlasting love. All things are Yours, and You are a generous God! I am Yours, and You are mine! Teach my heart to trust You today, and destroy the false idols and comforts in my life that are not of You. Amen.

Seek Christ as your hiding place.

DAY 10: BECOME UNSHAKEABLE

I have set the Lord always before me; because he is at my right hand, I shall not be shaken.

Psalm 16:8

The ground beneath us was shaking, yet we had no idea why. Later, on the news, we heard that the hunches we'd had about something being not quite right were correct. Although it was small in magnitude, an earthquake had unexpectedly barreled through our town, leaving all of us a little on edge.

The earth can be shaken at any time, without warning. And so can we. We shake when we're cold, when we're nervous, and when we have a fever. In fact, shaking is part of our built-in flight or flight messaging system. When danger comes, our bodies flood with the pure energy of adrenaline, causing us to become anxious and even shudder. Can you think of a time when your body was physically shaking from anxiety? Can you remember the danger you felt?

David's words in Psalm 16 were so relevant to the human walk of faith that the apostle Peter referenced them hundreds of years later in his first sermon to the early church. All generations of God's children have been jolted by circumstances they couldn't see coming. Yet

David reminds us that setting the Lord before us ensures that we will not be shaken.

Situations have the power to rattle us to the core, but with God we can remain still in His presence, unshaken. When you face a day full of panic, remember that He has gone before you, and He is at your right hand.

GO DEEPER

1. Is your mind intently fixed on God during unexpected difficulties or times of stress? Meditate on being still in God's presence from Psalm 16.

_____

_____

_____

_____

_____

_____

_____

_____

_____

_____

_____

GO DEEPER

2. Journal a few words to describe how it feels to be unshaken, resting in the arms of God.

_____

_____

_____

_____

_____

_____

_____

_____

_____

_____

_____

_____

_____

_____

_____

_____

_____

Dear sovereign God, I ask You today to keep my mind intently fixed on You. Help me to focus on Your presence so that when I am in distress, I will feel Your hand guiding me and drawing me back into Your loving arms. Thank You, Lord, that, as Your beloved child, I do not have to face my days with fear. No matter what trouble comes, You have promised that I can be still and remain unshaken. Shelter me in Your arms — be my refuge and strength, a very present help in trouble. Be my mountain — a rock that cannot be moved but abides forever. As I see Your mountains and strong walls surrounding me, let me be reminded that You surround Your people with strength and love. Amen.

As a child of God, you can remain steady, safe, and unshaken.

SECTION THREE
OVERCOMING ANXIETY

Even though I walk through the valley of the shadow of death, I will fear no evil, for you are with me.

Psalm 23:4a

When anxiety suddenly overtakes you, how do you react? How do you make it leave? How do you protect your thoughts to keep anxiety from coming back again?

In Section 3, you'll practice how to build your trust on the unshakeable foundation of Jesus. You'll start by examining how your anxiety and worries reveal where you are currently putting your trust. You'll name your anxieties to God and use them to refocus on your true source of peace. You'll seek out and abide in God's house as the safe place that shelters you from worry.

DAY 11: TRUSTING GOD

Rejoice in the Lord always; again I will say, rejoice. Let your reasonableness be known to everyone. The Lord is at hand; do not be anxious about anything, but in everything by prayer and supplication with thanksgiving let your requests be made known to God. And the peace of God, which surpasses all understanding, will guard your hearts and your minds in Christ Jesus.

Finally, brothers, whatever is true, whatever is honorable, whatever is just, whatever is pure, whatever is lovely, whatever is commendable, if there is any excellence, if there is anything worthy of praise, think about these things. What you have learned and received and heard and seen in me—practice these things, and the God of peace will be with you.

Philippians 4:4-9

The Bible is a gold mine of practical tips that will decrease your anxiety. You may have noticed that today's Scripture passage is a little longer than usual. That's intentional. The most practical aid we can look to in our distress is the unfailing Word of God. Take your time as you read this passage from Philippians again, presenting all of your thoughts and worries to the Lord.

Anxiety and worry can show us the counterfeit and misleading objects of our trust. Today, do not focus on getting rid of your worry, but on probing it to learn more about the unreliable things you put your trust in. You may not always feel in complete control of your anxious thoughts, but you can change what you believe about them. Extend grace to yourself as you ask God to be the only object of your trust.

GO DEEPER

1. What are you afraid of in this very moment? Where does your trust lie?

_____

_____

_____

_____

_____

_____

_____

_____

_____

_____

_____

_____

_____

GO DEEPER

2. List some of your past and present fears and construct worst-case scenarios of your most dreaded fears coming true. Could you survive? Probe for any counterfeit and misleading people, places, and things where you have placed your trust that could be causing your anxiety. Where is God in these scenarios?

_____

_____

_____

_____

_____

_____

_____

_____

_____

_____

_____

_____

_____

_____

_____

_____

Lord God, my anxiety often causes spiraling thoughts and sleepless nights. Help me to remember that You are my one true comfort. Help me to never forget that You are always with me. Help me to know that You will never leave me. When I realize that my anxieties and fears are covered by You, then what else is left to fear? Help me to replace those unreliable things that make my anxiety worse with thoughts that draw me closer to You. In Jesus' name. Amen.

God desires all of your trust, not just part of it.

DAY 12: NAME YOUR ANXIETY

Humble yourselves, therefore, under the mighty hand of God so that at the proper time he may exalt you, casting all your anxieties on him, because he cares for you.

1 Peter 5:6-7

The first thing you do when you introduce yourself to someone new is tell them your name. Whether you share a name with your great-great-grandfather or you go by a nickname from school, your name is one of the most important things about you. It helps everyone else in your life to mentally file away information about you and your life, and it allows them to know who you are apart from everyone else.

The same is true with anxiety. If you don't name it, call it out, and set it apart, it will get jumbled in with the rest of your thoughts, lost somewhere between your favorite childhood memories and everyday queries like, "What should we have for dinner?" and leave behind an uneasiness that seeps into everything. While you may be unable to name the specific threat or danger that is causing your anxiety, slowing down enough to label the feeling itself signals that you won't be running from it any longer.

Maybe your legs didn't even feel like they had been running, but your mind hasn't seen rest in far too long. Calling out your anxiety allows you to see what it truly is. Naming it provides a clarity to discern the truth from the lies. Begin today by naming the emotions you feel, no matter what they are. Hold them up to the truth and promises of Christ. May He shower you with clarity and unexpected peace today.

GO DEEPER

1. Identify the emotions you are feeling now or have felt today. Acknowledge each of them by name.

GO DEEPER

2. Identify the promises God gives you in 1 Peter 5:6-7.
    Meditate on these as you bring your emotions before
    God and replace your worries with His truths.

_____

_____

_____

_____

_____

_____

_____

_____

_____

_____

_____

_____

_____

_____

_____

_____

Lord God, You knew we would struggle with fear. You anticipated that we would have sleepless nights. And, in those times, You knew we would benefit from the gift of Your Word, Your Spirit, and Your presence in prayer. We ask now boldly for moments of peace today. Interrupt our runaway emotions with Your divine presence. Break through our fears and anxiety today and give us a calm heart as You remind us of who You are, Your strength, Your help, and how You hold us in Your hands. In Jesus' name. Amen.

Name your anxieties, for the one who calls you by name cares for you.

DAY 13: SEEK REFUGE IN GOD

I will say to the Lord, "My refuge and my fortress, my God, in whom I trust."
Psalm 91:2

If you suffer from a fear of dinner parties, you may have deipnophobia. If you always wear pants, even on the hottest day of the year, it may be because you have genuphobia, or a fear of knees. And if you have sesquipedalophobia, hopefully you aren't reading this, since you have a fear of long words.

Everyone has a silly phobia that they are embarrassed to admit. I, for one, have nightmares about ostriches, while my friend has a more realistic fear of flying. We all at times also have extreme fears that keep us awake at night — fears of losing a loved one, illness, loneliness, or death itself. We live in a world where it seems that our worst fears could come true without any notice. This is exactly why we need God. Knowing that we live in a current of pain and suffering, we need to know that Christ gives us a hiding place, a shelter from the storm, and a refuge from the raging tides.

Maybe you find yourself in a place you never imagined you would be and you can't see your way out. Maybe you're walking through the trials of a friend and you're out of encouragement to give. You are never too far away or too far gone to stand under the covering of Christ. He does not promise us a life without fear or pain or trouble, but He does promise us refuge in Himself. And when we receive His love, we know this is more than enough.

GO DEEPER

1. Journal a few words to describe how it would feel to find safety from your greatest fears in a place of refuge.

_____

_____

_____

_____

_____

_____

_____

_____

_____

_____

_____

_____

_____

2. What is your reaction to the knowledge that you are
    promised both temporary suffering and eternal life in Christ?

    _____

    _____

    _____

    _____

    _____

    _____

    _____

    _____

    _____

    _____

    _____

    _____

    _____

    _____

    _____

    _____

    _____

Dear God, Psalm 91 says that You give Your angels orders to protect me, and they will hold me with their hands. What a powerful thing to remember. You, Lord, are my refuge. You are a strong tower that will never fall. When I abide in You, I find safety. You don't promise that I will never experience fear or suffering, but You do give me strength and peace as I battle through life's trials. No matter what is happening around me, I have hope in an eternal future with You. Help me to have confidence in You. Give me Your perspective so that I can see beyond the fear and pain of the here and now. Grant me faith to believe that You will use my circumstances and experiences for Your good purpose and Your great glory. Amen.

God promises to never leave you in your fear.

DAY 14: ABIDE IN GOD'S HOUSE

The Lord is my light and my salvation;
whom shall I fear?
The Lord is the stronghold of my life;
of whom shall I be afraid?
When evildoers assail me
to eat up my flesh,
my adversaries and foes,
it is they who stumble and fall.
Though an army encamp against me,
my heart shall not fear;
though war arise against me,
Yet I will be confident.
One thing have I asked of the Lord,
that will I seek after:
that I may dwell in the house of the Lord
all the days of my life,
to gaze upon the beauty of the Lord
and to inquire in his temple.
For he will hide me in his shelter
in the day of trouble;
he will conceal me under the cover of his tent;
he will lift me high upon a rock.
And now my head shall be lifted up
above my enemies all around me,
and I will offer in his tent
sacrifices with shouts of joy;

I will sing and make melody to the Lord.

Psalm 27:1-6

We don't know exactly how anxious the prophet David was before he uttered the words of Psalm 27, but we can guess. This psalm teaches us a very important truth about anxious thoughts — they lead us to our need for Christ. Notice David's deep desire in the face of his anxiety — he wants to live in the house of the Lord, contemplate His beauty, and study at His feet. Today, join David in trading your temporary worries for praises of God's eternal glory.

GO DEEPER

1. Which behaviors do you need to remove from your life and which behaviors do you need to add to your life to live at peace and free from anxiety in the house of the Lord? Write them down. Confess them to God now.

GO DEEPER

2. Choose one of the details in Psalm 27 to focus on today. Which one stands out to you the most? Why?

_____

_____

_____

_____

_____

_____

_____

_____

_____

_____

_____

_____

_____

_____

_____

_____

_____

_____

_____

Lord God, today I pray the words of David. I too am eager to enter into Your house and live in Your eternal kingdom. Lord, I can't wait until the day when I won't ever forget to contemplate Your beauty and study at Your feet. Please remove any distractions and negative behavior in my life that distract me from the good work You are doing in my life. Provide me with community to keep me accountable for these changes that glorify You, for I know they may be difficult. Thank You for seeing my weaknesses and still loving me. Lord, show me Your peace as I put my faith, hope, and trust in You to transform me to be more like You. In Your Son's name. Amen.

God shelters you when you abide in His house.

DAY 15: STAY FOCUSED ON JESUS

... looking to Jesus, the founder and perfecter of our faith, who for the joy that was set before him endured the cross, despising the shame, and is seated at the right hand of the throne of God.

Hebrews 12:2

When you look at a photograph, there is usually one thing that stands out the most — maybe it's a person, an animal, or an object. It's hard to see all of the details behind that one stand-out thing because they are usually blurrier than the object in focus. A seasoned photographer knows how to control the object of focus when taking a photo. Focus can make or break any photo.

The same is true about your mindset — focusing on the right or wrong thoughts can make all the difference between peace and anxiety. Reducing your symptoms of anxiety can begin with reframing your mental interpretation of your circumstances and your feelings about them. Changing your spiritual focus affects the way you experience your life, as well as the way you experience God. Christ came to replace anxiety with peace as the central focus of your life.

Here are some practical ways to refocus your mindset

when anxiety feels out of control:

- Prayer and communion with God
- Reading the truths found in God's Word
- Staying in fellowship with other believers
- Identifying your anxiety and anxiety triggers by name
- Replacing your anxious thoughts with God's promises

Anxious thoughts may still loom and blur in the background of your mind and your life from time to time, but with Christ as the object of your focus, you can know peace in Him.

GO DEEPER

1. If you could eliminate the most frightening situation in your life, what would it be?

_____

_____

_____

_____

_____

_____

_____

_____

GO DEEPER

2. There may be several, but name the messages, people, or events that trigger your anxiety. Confess these to God now. Ask God to help you exchange them for His truth and peace.

_____

_____

_____

_____

_____

_____

_____

_____

_____

_____

_____

_____

_____

_____

_____

_____

Lord God, You are the great healer. Heal me from my unruly anxiety, worry, confusion, fear, and concerns that keep me from You and Your peace. Lord God, help me to realize that You are with me and that You are working in me to make me whole. You promise to never leave me or forget me. Let me be free from anxiety and rest in Your presence. Your Word promises that You chose me and began a good work in me. Let me be free from worry, knowing always that I am chosen and loved. You promise that You will continue to do Your good work in me until Christ returns. May I live free from fear in this assurance. In the name of Jesus. Amen.

Keep your focus fixed on Christ.

SECTION FOUR
GOD IS WITH YOU IN SUFFERING

Just like anxiety, suffering can appear at your doorstep uninvited and unwanted. It can come without warning, seeming to destroy almost everything you.care about, and then have the audacity to stick around for a very, very long time. Where are You, God, when this suffering comes? Why do You let this happen to me? Do You really care about me?

Suffering may be one of the hardest things you face. It may even define big parts of who you are. Jesus faced the deepest suffering on the cross. He suffered for you to give you new life. This profound truth of the gospel changes everything about suffering. God understands the suffering you're going through. He has already walked through it Himself, and He wants to walk with you through it now to give you hope and the power to overcome.

In this section, with your companion Jesus, you'll seek hope and strength for the biggest storms of your life. You can be honest with God about the pain, grief or disappointment that you face. You can train to walk through suffering with Jesus — even when you must let Him carry you down the path — so you can come out secure in His love and renewed by His Spirit.

DAY 16: SUFFER WITH GOD

The Lord is near to all who call on him, to all who call on him in truth. He fulfills the desire of those who fear him; he also hears their cry and saves them.

Psalm 145:18-19

There are some forms of communication that require you to physically be in a certain location to receive a message. Walkie-talkies, for one, need two people to remain within a certain number of feet from each other. If you have a landline phone, you won't receive any calls unless you are in your home. But, in these days filled with more technology than we know what to do with, we can usually reach anyone, no matter where that person is or how many miles are between us.

Do you ever feel that maybe you are not standing in the right place to make contact with God, like He's out of reach or out of town, gone for the evening with friends, or just not answering?

In the depths of suffering, it's easy to believe that God is far away and will not be able to rescue you; but the truth is, He is near every time you call to Him. All God asks is that your cries to Him be filled with truth, without hiding who you are from who He is, and without fear or seeking who you are apart from Him. If you're calling God for comfort, He is near. If you're crying to Him for clarity, He is near. If you're calling Him filled with confusion, He is still near. Whenever His children call, He is near.

Call out to the Lord today. He will hear you.

GO DEEPER

1. Where do you think God is when you cry out to Him? As you practice calling out to Him today, visualize Him moving toward you as you speak.

_____

_____

_____

_____

_____

_____

_____

_____

_____

_____

_____

_____

_____

GO DEEPER

2. Where do you turn when trouble comes? Is it to God? Scripture? Prayer? Something else? Someone else? How can you call out confidently today, knowing that God is close?

_____

_____

_____

_____

_____

_____

_____

_____

_____

_____

_____

_____

_____

_____

_____

_____

_____

Heavenly Father, thank You for being here with me. No matter where I go, You promise to be near. You are glory and holiness, yet You still listen to my requests and answer them with love and compassion. Lord, You know my heart, and You know my life. You see me. I ask You now to save me from this suffering I feel. Please show me mercy and grant me peace. In the midst of all this uncertainty and pain, I pray that You would open my eyes and help me to see that You will never leave me. Help me to see the ways You are working in my life. I offer and pray this in Your holy name. Amen.

God is nearby to help you and hear you.

DAY 17: JESUS, A MAN DESPISED

He was despised and rejected by men, a man of sorrows and acquainted with grief; and as one from whom men hide their faces he was despised, and we esteemed him not.

Isaiah 53:3

Read these words slowly, holding the weight of their truth in your heart. Allow the scene to unfold in your mind. Men hid their faces from Him, yet His own expressions remained unhidden and tell us a story filled with sorrow and grief. Jesus was not held in any kind of esteem, but He continued to stand unmoved in His pain, revealing the highest level of care and love for us. He did this because He was not just carrying the tears of His own sadness to the cross — He was holding the hurts of your heartaches, too.

He felt a specific sorrow — the one you fear nobody will understand.
He knew a certain grief — the one that sometimes makes you feel alone.

Men hid their faces from Him, not knowing it was the only place to find peace. Jesus did not come for power. He is power. He did not come to be flattered. He is glory itself. He came to be a despised man to solidify your place as His beloved child. He suffered alone to ensure that you would not.

Do you cling to the truth of the gospel in your suffering?
Ask God now to help you to not be overwhelmed by the
waves of disaster around you and to stand unmoved,
trusting in God's promises. May the weight of His sacrifice
cause your heart to feel relief today.

GO DEEPER

1. What do you want the most — for the hard stuff to
   become easy, or to be unmoved in your faith when the
   hard stuff comes? Why is this the case?

_____

_____

_____

_____

_____

_____

_____

_____

_____

_____

_____

_____

_____

GO DEEPER

2. Write about one way Jesus gives you purpose in your suffering. Why does it matter to you that He is a God who has experienced suffering?

_____

_____

_____

_____

_____

_____

_____

_____

_____

_____

_____

_____

_____

_____

_____

_____

Jesus, I am grateful that You are God. You were there when the foundations of the earth were laid, and You are king in heaven now. You stepped off Your glorious throne and came down to earth where You knew You would be despised, rejected, and forsaken. You knew You would suffer and experience sorrow and pain, yet You came anyway because You also knew You would fulfill a promise: to break the barrier between us and God so that we can sit right now as Your children in Your presence. You are Lord of my life; let me never forget Your great value. Thank You for Your sacrifice, the greatest display of love I will ever know. Amen.

Jesus was despised so that you could be eternally loved.

DAY 18: ENDURING DIFFICULT TIMES

Rejoice in hope, be patient in tribulation, be constant in prayer.
Romans 12:12

You may not have woken up this morning believing you
could run a marathon. But the truth is, no one is actually
born a marathoner. Rather, you must train long and hard
before the big race — strengthening your muscles, building
your stamina, and lengthening your endurance. You have
to run hundreds of miles before the day of the race,
practicing and sweating until you finally achieve the
unimaginable.

As a follower of Christ, running twenty-six point two miles
can seem like a small feat compared to the sufferings we
are called to endure in this life. To prepare for suffering,
God calls us to train long and hard, too, to practice our
heart's correct posture even before we feel the first twinge
of pain. He wants our souls to remember where to turn
when the storms rage and how to stay calm in the storms.
Thankfully, Paul gave us specific directions for building our
endurance in Romans 12:

You must train your hope to rejoice.
You must train tribulation to link arms with patience.
You must train your prayer to be constant.

Saint Francis de Sales once said, "Every one of us needs half an hour of prayer a day, except when we are busy — then we need an hour." It's the same when we are facing trials — we need God more. In suffering, our muscles may not naturally run to joy, but they can learn to run to Christ, our constant source of hopeful endurance. May He steady us with His presence, allowing us to endure what we could not bear alone.

GO DEEPER

1. Do you joyfully lean into Jesus during difficult times or do you grumble impatiently?

2. What is the current status of your training for suffering? Is your endurance level high enough that you are able to rejoice in hope, be patient in tribulation, and be constant in prayer? If not, what do you still need to do?

Dear enduring God, You know my heart and are intimately aware of my circumstances, even more than I am. In my difficult days, please help me to find peace. Show me the paths that lead to You and not away from You. Even in the midst of a commotion of uncertainty, may the love I feel for You be sincere and active. When I face hard times, grant me the courage to hate what is evil and hold on tightly to what is good. Show me what it means to feel calm, not because of my circumstances, but because of Your enduring presence. Let Your Spirit knit into me an awareness of constant and rejoicing hope — the hope that gives me reassurance in Christ and compels me to lean into Him. May I stay devoted to prayer, continually seeking Your wisdom, guidance, and strength. In Your holy name I pray. Amen.

Your endurance comes from Christ who steadies you with His presence.

DAY 19: STANDING FIRM IN SUFFERING

And after you have suffered a little while, the God of all grace, who has called you to his eternal glory in Christ, will himself restore, confirm, strengthen, and establish you.

1 Peter 5:10

Not even my sturdiest pair of hiking boots can make me feel like I am standing on solid ground in times of suffering. It's usually quite the opposite — when pain starts, I panic. I'm more likely to lace up my running shoes to escape grief's ache or tiptoe around in my bare feet, pretending to ignore fear's what-ifs. You too? I look for anything, even a pair of warm socks, to guarantee me some around-the-clock comfort. But God never promises us comfort.

The places He asks us to plant our feet — in our trials and hardships, losses and disappointments, hurts and discomfort — are never ones we would choose for ourselves. We cannot forget that.

It is not the stamina of your own two legs or the sturdiness of your shoes that allows you to remain upright and strong in your seasons of suffering. *Standing firm requires solid ground.* It is the enduring hope of Christ's eternal glory that enables you to stand firm. Regardless of your present circumstances, the soil beneath you is packed with strength and care from your Creator, the God of all grace who holds everything together, just as He holds you close. On this solid ground, He restores, confirms, strengthens, and establishes you as His child. On this solid ground, may you find yourself both more and more incapable without Him and more and more hopeful in Him. On this solid ground, you can stand firm with Christ and firm in suffering.

Focus on the many ways He is with you today.

GO DEEPER

1. There are four action words in this verse — restore, confirm, strengthen, and establish. Choose one to meditate on, asking God to show you where and how He is accomplishing this in your life.

_____

_____

_____

_____

_____

_____

_____

_____

_____

2. Visualize yourself standing on the ground of today's hardships. How does seeing Christ standing with you change the picture?

_____

_____

_____

_____

_____

_____

_____

_____

_____

_____

_____

_____

_____

_____

_____

_____

_____

Lord God, I am weak. In my own strength, I try to face the trials that come my way, but I fail so often. On my own, I stand, only to fall back down. Today, as I face suffering that feels impossible to withstand, help me to remember the eternal glory You have called me to in Christ. In the midst of all the pain and uncertainty, please help my mind rest in reminders of Your care for me. Restore my hope. Confirm my faith. Strengthen my flesh. Establish me firmly in the truth of who You are. Amen.

You can stand firmly in suffering when you stand on solid ground with Christ.

DAY 20: SUFFER WELL

For Christ also suffered once for sins, the righteous for the unrighteous, that he might bring us to God, being put to death in the flesh but made alive in the spirit...

1 Peter 3:18

God, help me. Jesus, save me. Lord, make it stop. Heal me. Restore me. Comfort me. Bring an end to this, God!

Do these cries sound familiar? You've probably whispered (or yelled) a few of them to God in your suffering.

Maybe you've even pleaded: *Why is there suffering? Why me? Why this? Why now?*

Keep these cries and pleas near. Continue to seek God in them. But, just for this moment, allow yourself to ask Him a different question: *What would it look like for me to suffer well?*

"Well" is a word that can mean many things. Usually, it means something like "in a satisfactory manner." Doing well at your job can mean climbing the corporate ladder to the corner office. In school, it could mean studying hard and getting an A on a final exam. But these are definitions that imply an aggressive action — they require you to move, initiate, and follow through.

Please don't let these kinds of experiences of doing well

in daily life sway you into believing that suffering well requires the same action on your part. In spiritual growth, the moving, initiating, and following through has already been accomplished and completed in Christ.

Suffering well means aggressively choosing to rest in hope, abide in faith, and trust in God. It means seeking life in the Spirit that He has already given us. Jesus suffered well for us. May we give Him thanks and follow His lead.

GO DEEPER

1. When you suffer, what is the state of your heart? Are you able to suffer well?

_____

_____

_____

_____

_____

_____

_____

_____

_____

GO DEEPER

2. Journal a few words to describe how you typically want
    to be rescued. From what? To what? How do you think
    God defines rescue?

Dear heavenly Father, thank You for being sovereign over us and bigger than the sufferings we face. Lord, it is easy to look at the suffering in our world and question You. I wonder how You could allow it, why You would let it happen, why You haven't stopped it. There is so much suffering that I don't understand. I need You to give me the strength to lean on You and find comfort in that. Teach me what it means to suffer well, specifically in the struggles I face today. Remind me of the ways You suffered well and show me how to trust in You and follow in Your path. In Your name. Amen.

You can suffer well because Christ did it first.

SECTION FIVE
GOD PROTECTS AND PROVIDES

*"You are my servant, I have chosen you and not cast
you off; fear not, for I am with you; be not dismayed,
for I am your God; I will strengthen you, I will help you,
I will uphold you with my righteous right hand."*
Isaiah 41:9b-10

For the last twenty days, you have been practicing
finding refuge from the daily storms of anxiety and
the big storms of suffering. Hopefully, you have seen
how God walks with you through your trials, offering
hope and healing. God wants to free you from anxiety
so you can accomplish greater things than you can
think, ask, or imagine.

Over the next ten days, you will focus on becoming
equipped for God's bigger plans and purpose. To do
this, you will need to put on God's armor and step
into bold prayers of faith. The power of God's
protection not only lets you be safe, but it gives you
the confidence to pursue His plans for your life.

Let's begin by putting on the full armor of God.

DAY 21: THE ARMOR OF GOD

Finally, be strong in the Lord and in the strength of his might.
Ephesians 6:10

Last week, without any warning, the gas pedal in my car decided to give out. Unfortunately, this didn't happen within the safe confines of a parking lot or a deserted street — it was on the interstate during rush hour. *Of course.*

It's embarrassing to get stuck on the highway, watching all the other cars fly past without stopping to offer any assistance. But the fact is, we didn't break down because of something we forgot to take care of or a skill we failed to master — breakdowns happen. It's just life being life, simply one of the many storms we will face as human beings, even if we are a child of Christ.

Life is unpredictable. Some days, we feel unbelievably strong, like we could go full-force without stopping, above the speed limit, and without getting caught. No trouble in sight. Then, other days, the storm clouds roll in and bury us, making it a lot harder to even get on the road. We're stuck, flattened, and unable to move ahead at all.

Chapter 6 of Ephesians is perhaps the clearest picture of the storms we live in. It not only assures us that there is a spiritual war being waged around us, but it warns us that apart from utilizing the weapons that God has provided for us, we are hopelessly ill-equipped and underpowered.

In a world of go-getters and try-harders, it's easy to feel set back by reminders of our weakness. Relief only comes when we realize that we are not capable of stopping the downpour, but we can stand under the covering of a God who is sovereign and perfect. Face today knowing that He has equipped you mightily with His love and protection.

GO DEEPER

1. What weapons are you currently using to fight against the world? How effective are they?

_____

_____

_____

_____

_____

_____

_____

_____

_____

_____

GO DEEPER

2. In what areas of your life do you feel ill-equipped and underpowered? Write a prayer inviting God into those areas today.

_____

_____

_____

_____

_____

_____

_____

_____

_____

_____

_____

_____

_____

_____

_____

_____

_____

Dear strong and mighty God, shield me from the raging storms of this world. Protect me with Your power, Your defenses, and Your strength. Thank You that through Your presence, I am strong. I know that in You I draw my strength and continue to be empowered through my union and relationship with You. Your laws, commands, and precepts are like the splendid armor of a heavily armed soldier. As I wear the protective armor You have given me, help me to feel Your endless power. Remind me of Your peace and assurance. With Your armor, I can successfully stand up against anything that tries to keep me from You and Your truth. I know my struggle is not against flesh and blood or physical opponents, but against the rulers and powers of this present darkness. Against them, help me to stand firm in my place, fully prepared, immovable, victorious in Your name and by Your might. And for these things, I give You thanks. Amen.

With God on your side, you are never underpowered or weak.

DAY 22: STANDING STRONG

Put on the whole armor of God, that you may be able to stand against the schemes of the devil.

Ephesians 6:11

One of my friends cannot go to sleep without making sure a baseball bat is securely resting at the top of the stairs. I'm not sure how she plans to use it, or if she even has a plan, or if it's fear or practicality that drives her to keep it there, but I do know that it helps her rest easier at night. Isn't it funny the things that we do just to feel safe?

Although you may not have the same nightly routine, are there questions you need answers to so that you can sleep soundly and weather through the unknown? Questions like: Am I safe? Am I strong? Am I enough?

As a child of God, you haven't just been given the answers to these questions; you get to tangibly wear them for protection.

Read through each piece of God's armor and imagine what it feels like to put it on yourself, adding each layer of protection to the circumstances of your day.

The belt of truth.
The breastplate of righteousness.

Shoes of the gospel of peace.
The shield of faith.
The helmet of salvation.

In His armor, you are safe and strong because He is enough. When you hear the rumble of storm clouds, stop and diligently put on each piece of God's armor, then walk forward in confidence, knowing that His armor will protect you.

As you face the dark clouds and anxious tides that surround you today, know you are kept safe in the hands of God.

GO DEEPER

1. Which piece of God's armor makes you feel the safest? Why?

_____

_____

_____

_____

_____

_____

_____

_____

2. Which piece of God's armor may need more reinforcement today? Why? What can you do to reinforce each piece of God's armor?

_____

_____

_____

_____

_____

_____

_____

_____

_____

_____

_____

_____

_____

_____

_____

_____

_____

_____

Dear sovereign God, it is no surprise to You that I am weak and in need of Your strength. Alone, I am helpless against the attacks of darkness, but You replace every broken piece in my arsenal of protection with something stronger. Today, please help me to stop trying to fight the darkness on my own. Arm me with the belt of truth and the breastplate of righteousness. Help me to stand firmly, knowing I have the shoes of the gospel of peace and the shield of faith to protect me. Crown my head with the helmet of salvation, and seal my heart with thankfulness for the armor You have given me. Thank You for being strong when I am not and for always desiring my good. It is in Jesus' holy and strong name I pray for Your grace and protection. Amen.

God has given you everything you need to be safe.

DAY 23: POWERFUL PRAYERS OF FAITH

Ah, Lord God! It is you who have made the heavens and the earth by your great power and by your outstretched arm! Nothing is too hard for you.

Jeremiah 32:17

There are some things that are too hard for me. At the top of my list are lighthearted things like unicycling, sticking to a strict diet, and remembering to take laundry out of the dryer. But if I kept going down my list, there are more unbearable things like grief, anxiety, and dark days that never see the sunshine. What about you — what things are too hard for you?

This question can lead to an overwhelming list in no time. The prophet Jeremiah probably felt this way, too. There was nothing easy about His calling and nothing popular about His message. But this did not stop him.

After you compile your list of things that seem hard, or even impossible, instead of wallowing in the gloom of your circumstances, look to God's list: there is nothing on it! *Nothing. Absolutely nothing is too hard for Him.*

This is the proper posture of prayer — remembering again and again who your Creator is and what He can do and has already done. He made the heavens and the earth by His great power and by His outstretched arm. Knowing and believing in Him and His mighty power, your own limited capabilities matter less and less.

Jeremiah righteously feared God, which led him to frequent prayer by faith, pressing into the God who is sovereign over all. Even when Jeremiah did not understand what God was doing, he trusted in who He is. May you do the same today.

GO DEEPER

1. What things did you list that seem too hard for you right now? What makes them so difficult? In what ways can you bring them to God?

_____

_____

_____

_____

_____

_____

_____

_____

_____

GO DEEPER

2. What does praying by faith mean to you? Write down
   something you want to pray boldly in faith.

_____

_____

_____

_____

_____

_____

_____

_____

_____

_____

_____

_____

_____

_____

_____

_____

_____

_____

Sovereign God, You created the earth and the galaxies with Your hands. You are king over the entire world; there is nothing You cannot do. You are in control of everything, including the times of my life that seem out of control to me. Help me to look for You in those hard times, dear God. Help me to gather wisdom and see You more clearly. Help me to press into You in faith, even when I don't understand what You are doing. May You work in such powerful ways that I will know it can only come from You. In Jesus' name. Amen.

Your prayers can be as bold and mighty as the God who hears them.

DAY 24: GOD'S PLANS WILL HAPPEN

"For I know the plans I have for you," declares the Lord, "plans for welfare and not for evil, to give you a future and a hope."
Jeremiah 29:11

I knew the 2017 total solar eclipse was coming, but I had no idea what to expect. Scientists, researchers, and reporters gave us fair warning and their best explanations to describe what would happen. A group of friends and I planned the whole day's events — we would gather in an open field to watch it together. But when the moment of totality actually came and we looked to the pitch-black sky in the middle of the day, nothing could have prepared us; we were completely awestruck!

Total darkness is not outside of God's plan. Jeremiah 29:11 is an often-quoted Bible verse that makes us believe that God's plans for us include only prosperity and health, which is great, until that is no longer your experience. Where is God then?

Jeremiah 29:11 was written to a people who were experiencing exile and hardship, people who actually would not see freedom for another generation. Suffering is not a mistake or a deviation from God's plan; it is a core element of it. It is an essential part of life that is actually needed to give you a future and hope.

Understanding God's promises is like glancing at a single star through a telescope — you cannot see the entire span of sky that is made up of both darkness and light. It is just as hard to draw conclusions about the entire span of life from the perspective of a single day or a single storm. To experience light and calm, we must also know what it means to experience darkness and storms. We need to experience both these extremes in order to see the one true constant — a God who keeps His promises.

GO DEEPER

1. Which of your own plans for your life have not succeeded as you had hoped? Where do you imagine God is during your troubled circumstances? Is that place different from where He is during your successes?

_____

_____

_____

_____

_____

_____

GO DEEPER

2. Describe your life in terms of light and calm and darkness and storms.

_____

_____

_____

_____

_____

_____

_____

_____

_____

_____

_____

_____

_____

_____

_____

_____

_____

_____

Sovereign God, You are the Alpha and Omega, the beginning and the end. It is so comforting to know that You have plans for me, even when I don't know which way to go. You have hope for me, even when I feel like I don't have any left. You have a future for me, even though getting through today seems too hard. You are present with me today, but You have also gone before whatever storms may come tomorrow. You have designed history so that it may bring You glory. You have created my life so that I may know You more. Help me to hope in these truths today and know that You hold me, just as You hold the future. In Your name. Amen.

God's plans for you are happening in bigger ways than you can see.

DAY 25: BE CONFIDENT IN GOD

But the Lord is faithful. He will establish you and guard you against the evil one.

2 Thessalonians 3:3

We are born unable to do anything for ourselves. When you were a baby, someone else had to feed you, hold you, and keep you safe. But, somewhere along the way, as you learned to take your first steps, feed yourself, and sleep through the night, your confidence in yourself grew; you may have even begun to believe you could accomplish anything.

What are you confident in today?
Is it your finances — your ability to provide?
Is it your successes — your ability to achieve?
Is it your relationships — your ability to love?

Imagine what would happen if all that was taken away. What if you could no longer provide, achieve, or do things for others? What would happen to your confidence then?

God doesn't have to try hard to be faithful; He is faithful. He doesn't have to try hard to remain in control; He controls all things.
God doesn't have to try hard to achieve success; He is perfect.

God doesn't have to try hard to love us; He is love.

Today's Scripture passage is from a letter that the apostle Paul wrote to the new church in Thessalonica. The Thessalonians believed that the end times were coming soon, causing them to be paralyzed with fear, to lose all confidence, and to see themselves as utterly helpless. Paul wrote the letter to encourage them and remind them of the things they could be confident in — God's faithfulness and protection. May this verse also encourage you as you pass through any uncertain storms ahead.

GO DEEPER

1. What do you have the most confidence in? Money? People? Things? Why are any of these worthy of your confidence?

_____

_____

_____

_____

_____

_____

_____

GO DEEPER

2. What is your biggest need today? How confident are you that God will provide what you need?

_____

_____

_____

_____

_____

_____

_____

_____

_____

_____

_____

_____

_____

_____

_____

Dear Lord Jesus, I know You are faithful. I know Your Word and teachings are true. I know You are able to strengthen me against all I face and that You are setting me on a firm foundation. I know You can protect and guard me from evil. Lord Jesus, I know these things, but it is often hard for me to believe them. Please help me with my unbelief. Give me the faith to have faith in who You are and Your love for me. Give me the hope to have hope. Give me the courage to be strong. Steer me away from human plans and human promises that are not of You, and keep me focused on You and You alone. Rest my confidence in nothing and no one but You and Your grace, Your power, Your mercy, and Your love. Amen.

The only sure place for your confidence to rest is in God who cares for you.

SECTION SIX
BE A PEACEMAKER

> *"Blessed are the peacemakers, for they will be called children of God."*
>
> Matthew 5:9 (NIV)

In our opening section of this devotional, we explored how Jesus does not just make peace; He is our peace. As you follow Christ more deeply, He shapes and molds you into an instrument of His peace. In these last five days, you will practice how to love in powerful, transforming ways that are only possible through the same love that Jesus first gave to you.

Lord, make me an instrument of Your peace:
where there is hatred, let me sow love;
where there is injury, pardon;
where there is doubt, faith;
where there is despair, hope;
where there is darkness, light;
where there is sadness, joy.

For it is in giving that we receive,
it is in forgiving that we are forgiven,
and it is in dying that we are born to eternal life.
(Saint Francis of Assisi)

DAY 26: MAKE PEACE THROUGH JESUS

So they took branches of palm trees and went out to meet him, crying out, "Hosanna! Blessed is he who comes in the name of the Lord, even the King of Israel!"
John 12:13

Every year, springtime comes to relieve us from the bleakness and cold of winter. Snow is exchanged for sunshine, freezing temperatures are replaced by flower beds, and evergreen trees are traded for Easter eggs.

But first comes Palm Sunday. A week before Easter, this high and holy day is observed with a procession of waving palm leaves to remind us of Jesus' triumphal entry into Jerusalem. But when we watch groups of actors reenact this event, we already know what happens next. The onlookers in the original crowd that day in Jerusalem did not know about the sacrifice Jesus would make barely a week later or how His sacrifice would lead them to eternity.

Imagine what it was like to be in the crowd that day, wondering what all the commotion was about. Jesus was a man who was known for speaking in small gatherings and for performing mysterious miracles. But this was different — He was triumphantly entering into Jerusalem on a donkey.

The people gathered, expecting a powerful king, but instead, they found a servant.

They expected to be freed from Roman persecution, but instead, they found a lamb coming to be sacrificed.

Christ did not just come to give us peace, He became our peace. May it not be only on Palm Sunday when you sing out, "Hosanna! Blessed is He who comes in the name of the Lord!" May you imitate Jesus and triumphantly be in the world as His servant peacemaker.

GO DEEPER

1. Imagine yourself in the crowd that day in Jerusalem. What is your response to seeing Jesus in this moment? What emotions does being there evoke in you?

_____

_____

_____

_____

_____

_____

_____

GO DEEPER

2. How can you imitate Jesus and live triumphantly in the world as His servant peacemaker?

_____

_____

_____

_____

_____

_____

_____

_____

_____

_____

_____

_____

_____

_____

_____

_____

_____

_____

Dear Lord, thank You for walking into my life. Your steps are humble and victorious, purposeful and affectionate. Today, I ask that You would help me to respond to You in my life in a way that is true, honoring, glorifying, and sincere. Some days, I lay down branches to You as my king. Many days, I shout "Hosanna!" joyfully and excitedly. Yet, there are other days that I ignore You, failing to see You walking right in front of me. Sometimes, I can't even look in Your eyes from my own guilt and shame. May I lay branches down before You, not for temporary earthly benefits but for eternal ones. May I follow You because You died for my sins, rose from the grave, and are coming back in power and glory to reign over all. Make me Your servant peacemaker, Lord. In Your name. Amen.

Jesus did not just come to make peace; He came to become your peace.

DAY 27: LOVE DEEPLY THROUGH JESUS

> *For the whole law is fulfilled in one word: "You shall love your neighbor as yourself."*
>
> Galatians 5:14

One of my friends once asked me a question that has forever changed the way I look at serving people: "How can I love you well during this?"

The circumstances I found myself in were treacherous with no calm end in sight. Honestly, I was confused by my friend's question because I had never been asked it before. How would you answer this same question for yourself today? No clichés or general answers allowed. Be specific. Jesus knows how to love well. Jesus' love for you is vast and wide, but it is also specific. He loves you, intimately and uniquely. Just as He knows exactly how to calm storms, He knows how to love you well in very specific ways.

Knowing this and reflecting on the ways you desire to be loved, how can this change the way you love others? Each and every one of your family, friends, and neighbors has a unique idea of the things that would make them feel well loved. In Christ, you have been given freedom to love well and be loved well, specifically, intimately, and uniquely.

It is easy to be concerned for others from a distance, but doing things for their immediate benefit requires hands and feet. It requires seeing a need and meeting it. It requires loving others so much that you don't just want them to feel loved by you, but you also want them to feel loved by the God who loves them freely, intimately, and uniquely, just as He created them.

GO DEEPER

1. How can you be intentional to show respect, love, and admiration to someone today?

_____

_____

_____

_____

_____

_____

_____

_____

_____

_____

_____

GO DEEPER

2. How is the message of love that Jesus lives different than the message the world gives?

_____

_____

_____

_____

_____

_____

_____

_____

_____

_____

_____

_____

_____

_____

_____

_____

_____

Jesus, You liberated us into freedom because You loved us. We were once enslaved to sin, and we could not think of anyone but ourselves, but, Lord Jesus, You gave us another way to live. Because of You, I can look out into the world and love others well with a selfless love that comes only from You. You love each one of us uniquely, intimately, and fully. Give me eyes to see the ways You specifically love me, Lord, and help me to see Your people the way You see them. Show me how to love them well. Help me to glorify Your name with every person I come in contact with today. I offer and pray this in the name of Jesus, Your Son, our Savior, and my Lord. Amen.

You were made to love deeply.

DAY 28: TO SERVE AS JESUS

"...even as the Son of Man came not to be served but to serve, and to give his life as a ransom for many."
Matthew 20:28

Jesus came to turn our world upside down in more ways than one. Throughout His ministry, we see Him doing the opposite of what was expected, acceptable, and customary. Some of the most astounding ways He did this were simply by showing the world who He was — a king who came to serve.

Dallas Willard said, "Blessed are the spiritual zeros — the spiritually bankrupt, deprived and deficient, the spiritual beggars, those without a wisp of 'religion'— when the kingdom of the heavens comes upon them."

Jesus teaches us this same idea — the first will be last, the last will be first, the most important will be the least, and the least important will become the most important. Even at the Last Supper, the disciples were fighting about who would sit next to Jesus. He wasn't just the most important person at the dinner; He was the most important person alive. And yet, He got up, wrapped a cloth around His waist, knelt down, and washed the disciples' feet. That should have been more than enough for the king who came to serve, but it was nothing compared to what He would do the next day — sacrifice everything for them.

Jesus, the Son of God, who was seated at the right hand of the Father in heaven, willingly and humbly stepped down from His rightful position to care for you. He performed the ultimate act of service by coming down into the rough waters of earth to love you. He became the ultimate picture of service so that you could do likewise and serve others.

GO DEEPER

1. Who in your life is serving you? How do you know more about Jesus because of them?

_____

_____

_____

_____

_____

_____

_____

_____

_____

_____

GO DEEPER

2. Make a goal for this week to serve someone anonymously. How does it feel to know you won't get credit?

_____

_____

_____

_____

_____

_____

_____

_____

_____

_____

_____

_____

_____

_____

_____

_____

_____

_____

_____

Dear heavenly Father, I confess I would rather be served than to serve. Sometimes, it's hard for me to see past myself, even when I have the best of intentions. Thank You for giving me the ultimate example of service and sacrifice through Your Son, who left His throne to become a lowly servant. I'm grateful that the way Your kingdom is designed is the opposite of the world I live in — where the last will be first, and the first will be last. Help me to adopt this mentality instead of the thoughts I am so quick to believe about being the first and the best. Guide me in my pursuits of serving others. Help me to see and love people, humbly and willingly, just as You pursue and love me. In Your name. Amen.

You serve others for the same reason Christ served — so that you will know Him more.

DAY 29: OVERCOME ANGER THROUGH JESUS

Be not quick in your spirit to become angry, for anger lodges in the heart of fools.

Ecclesiastes 7:9

I bet you usually lock the front door when you leave your house. Maybe you even have multiple locks, a gate, and an alarm system. Regardless, I think we can all agree that you care about keeping the things and people inside your home safe, from your shaggy dog to your sleeping relatives. But what if an unwelcome intruder has been secretly living there all along?

This is what anger is to our souls. Whether or not we ushered it in ourselves, when this toxic visitor rests in our hearts, it affects every part of our days.

I don't know who made Mark Twain angry, or if he was the one who started it, but I do know he said this: "Anger is an acid that can do more harm to the vessel in which it is stored than to anything on which it is poured." *Ouch.*

If you take so much care to safeguard where you physically live, shouldn't you do the same, if not more, to safeguard your spiritual house? Twain and Ecclesiastes 7:9 both point to the same human truth — *anger is a roadblock that prevents you from giving and receiving love from others, yourself, and God.*

The key to protecting your heart from intruders is not a strong defensive line or a collection of locks — it is slowing down, allowing your anger to be filtered through the Holy Spirit instead of through your own reactions. May you arm yourself with grace, love, and the presence of Christ the next time you feel anger.

GO DEEPER

1. When you are angry, do you feel yourself naturally slowing down or speeding up? Today, focus on slowing down to meditate on what is true.

2. Which negative feelings are taking up space in your soul today? Prayerfully bring each of them before God.

Father, help me to slow down. Open my heart to see any resentment or hurt that is keeping me from receiving Your love and hearing Your voice. I do not want to be the fool who allows anger to rest in my soul. Yet, many times, I discover that anger has been living in me for quite some time. Only by Your strength can I cease from anger and abandon wrath. Only by Your grace can I seek love instead of pride. When anger rises up in me, so quickly and unexpectedly, slow me down with reminders of Your truth. Give me greater understanding of my emotions so I can profit from self control. May I be quick to hear, slow to speak, and slow to anger (James 1:19). Amen.

Anger takes up space in your soul that was intended for love.

DAY 30: PRAY FOR YOUR ENEMIES

"But I say to you who hear, Love your enemies, do good to those who hate you, bless those who curse you, pray for those who abuse you."

Luke 6:27-28

You may have just read the title of today's meditation and want to skip to the end. You're not alone. Maybe it's because you don't feel ready to pray for your enemies, or because you believe you truly don't have any enemies.

Regardless of your feelings about praying for your enemies, don't dismiss them just yet. In this passage in Luke, Jesus doesn't say, "When you're ready, pray for your enemies." He also doesn't say, "*If* you happen to have enemies, pray for them." Instead, He says, "I say to you who hear, love your enemies."

In order to fully experience gospel transformation in your life, you must first admit you have enemies, then you have to love them. This is what Christ did for you — He faced sin, the thing He hated most, by performing the ultimate act of love and sacrifice. And that means you must also face the people you struggle with, using the most powerful tool you have — prayer.

Pastor T.D. Jakes once said, "I think the first step is to

understand that forgiveness does not exonerate the perpetrator; forgiveness liberates the victim."

Praying for, loving, blessing, and forgiving your enemies is muddy territory to walk in, but it is where Christ leads us. The purpose is not to let the other person win or to feel better than they are, but to experience Christ's peace through praying for your enemies. May you do so today.

GO DEEPER

1. Who in your life is the hardest person for you to pray for? Why? Meditate on praying for and blessing your enemies from Luke 6.

_____

_____

_____

_____

_____

_____

_____

_____

_____

_____

_____

GO DEEPER

2. Visualize the anger you feel toward someone — either currently or in the past. With your fists, practice gripping that anger and then letting it go. Meditate on Christ's forgiveness as you do so.

_____

_____

_____

_____

_____

_____

_____

_____

_____

_____

_____

_____

_____

_____

_____

_____

God of mercy, You love me unconditionally. You give me grace upon grace and call me Yours. You ask me to pray for and bless my enemies, and I confess that this is not easy. My heart holds bitterness, and most of the time I don't know what to do with it. Search my heart, dear God. Root out any trace of sinful hate and replace it with Your divine love instead. Give me the wisdom to know how to go about praying for my enemies in a fruitful, healthy way — whether that means reconciling with them or simply giving You the anger that eats away at my joy. Today, I pray for my enemies and ask that You would position our relationship so that it would glorify You. In Jesus' name. Amen.

You are God's ambassador to bring peace to your community.

WHAT'S NEXT

I hope that these 30 days have been marked by His presence, His power, and His truth. As you take the next steps in your journey, I invite you to consider the following:

- Seek daily refuge by committing to listen to Abide's daily meditation for the next 30 days.
- Remember one or two of your top highlights from this journaling devotional and share them with your family, friends, or someone from your church.
- Think of someone who can benefit from what you have experienced in this 30-day meditation on anxiety. Share a copy of this book with them.

May you ABIDE in the powerful presence of Jesus.

Blessings,
Kaitlin Wernet

Abide

Abide is the #1 Christian meditation app to bring more peace and less stress into your daily life. Transform your mind by listening to beautiful guided meditations. Join the millions of people meditating with Abide, including Grammy award-winning singers, church leaders, and well-known authors. It can be found on Google Play and iTunes.

CPSIA information can be obtained
at www.ICGtesting.com
Printed in the USA
LVOW04*1354300118
564581LV00009B/29/P